THE HONOR STUDENT AT MAGIC HIGH SCHOOL
Art Yu Mori
Original Story Tsutomu Sato
11
Character design Kana Ishida

CONTENTS

The Honor Student
at Magic High School

WE STILL HAVE THE MONOLITH CODE FINALS TOMORROW...
...BUT WITH OUR SCHOOL HAVING TAKEN FIRST PRIZE OVERALL IN THE NINE SCHOOL COMPETITION...
...LET'S TOAST!
わあっ
WAA (CHEER)
CONGRATS, MIYUKI!
THANK YOU FOR COMING, ERIKA!
WELL, YOU AND THE PRESIDENT DID KEEP INVITING ME...
CONGRATULATIONS, MIYUKI.
YOU WERE REALLY AMAZING!
THANK YOU.
HUH?
きょろ
KYORO (TURN)
KYORO
きょろ
WHERE'S TATSUYA-SAN?

CHAPTER 68

ONII-SAMA WENT TO BED EARLY.
HE WAS UNDER-STANDABLY TIRED.
WELL, HE *HAS* BEEN THE ONGOING STAR OF THE SHOW.
YES...
MIYUKI?
YES?
I KNOW YOU KNOW, BUT YOU'LL BE THE FOCUS OF THE PARTY LATER.
MEANING ...

I UNDERSTAND.
I'M ONLY HERE BECAUSE I WANTED TO SEE YOU OFF.
AH.
IT'S NOTHING MAJOR. I'LL BE BACK RIGHT AWAY.
なで
NADE (PET)

I'M SURE YOU'LL BE FINE, ONII-SAMA...
I WISH YOU LUCK...
THANKS, MIYUKI.

ONII-SAMA...
PLEASE STAY SAFE...

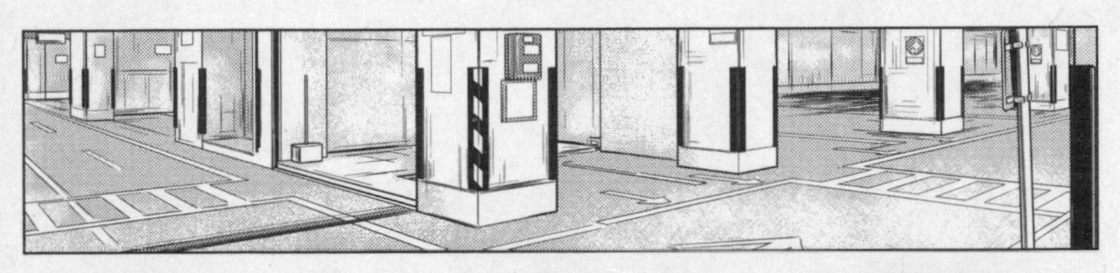

THANK YOU.
YOUR PAYMENT.
...!
IT'S MORE THAN ENOUGH. FOR... INSURANCE, RIGHT?
YES.

KACHI (CLICK)
カチ
KACHI
カチ

WHO WAS THAT?
MY SCHOOL GUIDANCE COUNSELOR—A PUBLIC SAFETY OPERATIVE.

THESE THINGS TEND TO GO BETTER WITH LESS EXPERIENCED PEOPLE.
...AND HOW OLD ARE YOU, EXACTLY ...?

THIS ENTIRE EXPERI-ENCE IS BEYOND MY STATION, THANK YOU.

......
HER SKILLS SEEM LEGIT.

LET'S HURRY.
YES, LET'S.

YOU SHOULD PROBABLY STILL BE RESTING.
JUST WHO DO YOU THINK I AM, SHIORI?
I'VE RESTED ENOUGH.

AND I REALLY WANT TO DO SOME MORE TESTS NOW.

YEAH, I GET THE FEELING!
MAGIC LIKE THIS DOESN'T COME AROUND TOO OFTEN.

HEY, I WANT TO TRY IT OUT TOO...

YOU WON'T BE ABLE TO LIKE THIS.
IT'S SET UP SPECIFICALLY FOR AIRI TO USE.
COME ON. JUST A LITTLE.
NO. IT'S DANGEROUS.
HMPH.

SORRY FOR BRINGING YOU OUT HERE.
NAW! I'D NEVER LET YOU PLAY AROUND WITH SUCH A FUN TOY ON THE SLY.
HEE HEE.

ポウ
POU
(GLOW)

ふわ
FUWARI
(FLOAT)

THE MARKERS ARE REALLY LIGHTING UP, HUH?
IT'S PRETTY.

DURING THAT MATCH...
...I REALIZED I COULD STILL...
...GO MUCH, MUCH FURTHER THAN MY CURRENT LIMITS.
THANK YOU...

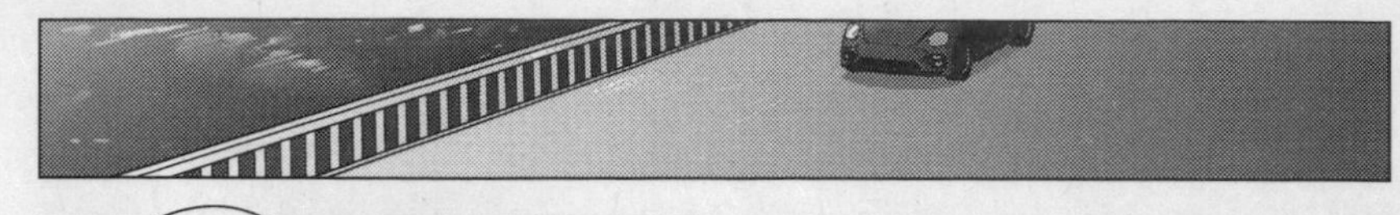

HACKING'S ALL DONE.

THE ELECTRON SORCERESS LIVES UP TO HER NAME.
I COULD NEVER IMITATE ALL THAT, NO MATTER HOW MUCH I FIDDLED WITH SPELLS.

THANK YOU.
WOULD BE A PROBLEM IF IT WERE EASY TO MIMIC, AFTER ALL.

CHA (CLICK)
LOOKS LIKE THE CABLES ARE CUT.
CAPTAIN SANADA HAS TAKEN CARE OF THEM.

KACHA (CHK)
カチャ

IT'S OVER A KILOMETER FROM HERE TO THE GRAND HOTEL.
BUT THAT'S NO ISSUE FOR HIM, IS IT...

DOSA
ドサドサ
DOSA (THUD)
BLAST! THEY'RE NOT GETTING AWAY WITH THIS!
JARA
ジャラ
JARA (JINGLE)
ジャラ
WE HADN'T EXPECTED THE IMPERIAL JAPANESE ARMY TO BRING OUT A SPECIAL UNIT FOR A MERE HIGH SCHOOL COMPETITION.
BASA (RUSTLE)
バサッ
AND NOW WE NEED TO FLEE IN THE NIGHT LIKE RATS!

ZUOOO
(ZHWRRR)
!!
BA
(FWIP)
GOO
(FOOM)

THE GENER-ATOR IGNITED AND VANISHED ...?
ARE WE UNDER ATTACK?
IN CA
RING RING RING
A PHONE CALL? NOW!?
THIS PHONE SHOULD ONLY BE CONNECTED TO HQ.
STILL...
RING RING
Howdy, No-Head Dragon.
Gentlemen of the main branch of eastern Japan...
A BOY ...?
...I must thank you for Fuji.

And so I've come to pay you back.
HUH!
!!
THE "AREA INTERFERENCE" FILTER PROTECTING THE ROOM IS GONE!?
OH NO! THE GENERATOR THAT WAS DEPLOYING THE SPELL—!

FANG
CHAPTER 69

ZAAAA (ZHHHH)
BOTH THE GENERATORS ARE DOWN...!
WHERE'S NUMBER 14!?
SU (POINT)
WHAT WAS THAT SPELL!?
THE BAY HILLS TOWER ...!?
FROM SO FAR!? HOW!?
IF I CAN JUST KILL THE MAGICIAN ...
THERE HE IS!
PIKU (TWITCH)
NI (SMIRK)

GWAAAAHHH!
FUCK, MY EYES!!
NUMBERS 14 AND 16, GET HIM!
CANNOT.
OUT OF RANGE.
DON'T TALK BACK TO ME! JUST DO IT!
AHHHH!
AHH...
AH!
AYEEE!
(VWP)
PL—
PLEASE WAIT!
WE WON'T INTERFERE ANY FURTHER! TOMORROW, WE'LL LEAVE THE COUNTRY!

No-Head Dragon will pull out of Japan!
DO YOU HAVE THE AUTHORITY TO MAKE THAT PROMISE?
IF YOU TWO ARE THAT CLOSE, THEN I'M SURE YOU'D KNOW THIS.
WHAT IS YOUR LEADER'S NAME, DOUGLAS HUANG?
I'm close with the boss! I've saved his life!
I...
HOW DID HE KNOW MY NAME?
He wouldn't ignore me!
AAHH!
JAMES !?
Was that James Zhu? I'll have to apologize to Interpol.
GAKU (SLUMP)
...THE BOSS'S NAME IS RICHARD SUN!

WHAT'S HIS PUBLIC NAME?
AND WHERE DOES HE LIVE?

FRE-QUENT ANY RESTAU-RANTS?
......
...

Thank you.
YOU'LL BELIEVE ME?
WHEW.
YEAH.
GAHHH!
GREGORY!

But why!? We haven't killed anyone!
IT DOESN'T MATTER TO ME HOW MANY YOU KILL.
YOU'VE LAID HANDS ON SOMETHING YOU NEVER SHOULD HAVE.
YOU'VE INCURRED MY WRATH.
THAT'S REASON ENOUGH TO ERASE EVERY LAST ONE OF YOU.

I WILL NEVER LET ANYTHING LIKE THAT HAPPEN...
...EVER AGAIN!

DAMN DEMON ...!
A DEMON... YEAH.
THANKS TO YOU DREDGING UP MY SINGLE EMOTION ...
...I'LL GET TO USE THE DEMON'S POWER FOR THE FIRST TIME IN A WHILE.
!!
THE DEMON'S POWER...?
WAIT, COULD THIS SPELL BE...
..."DEMON RIGHT"!?
ZWAH!

I TRUST THAT ONII-SAMA IS SAFE...
...BUT I CAN'T HELP WORRYING...

THE HONOR STUDENT AT MAGIC HIGH SCHOOL

CHAPTER 70
HEY, WANT TO GO TO THE BATHS AFTER THIS?
SURE.
WHAT ABOUT YOU, MIYUKI?
I SUPPOSE, AS LONG AS WE DON'T STAY TOO LATE.
IT'S DECIDED!
SIGN: BATHS
大浴場
LADIES
HUH!?

BUN (WAVE)
ぶん
OH! FANCY MEETIN' YOU HERE!
BUN
ぶん
YOU ALL TAKIN' A SOAK TOO?

THEY'RE ...
FROM THIRD HIGH...
WHAT TERRIBLE TIMING...
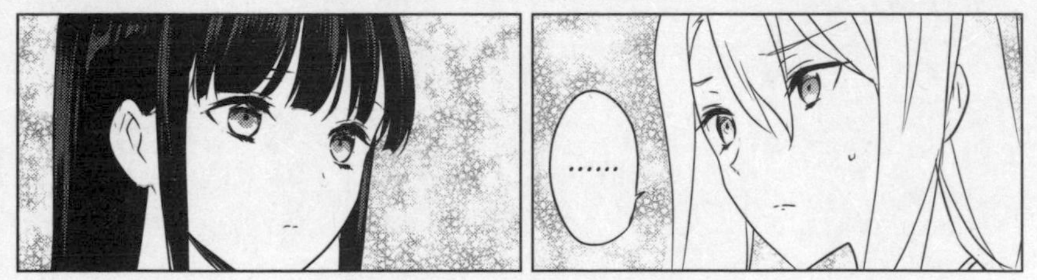
......

UGH, THIS IS AWK-WARD...
I MEAN, WE JUST COMPETED AGAINST THEM.
LET'S GET THIS OVER WITH QUICKLY.
ZAAAA (FSHHHH)
ACK! WHAT A PAIN!
?
MY HANDS WON'T REACH FAR ENOUGH TO WASH MY HAIR!
AT HOME, THE MAID ALWAYS DOES IT FOR ME!

AH, I KNOW! WON'T YOU HELP ME, MISSY?
PLEASE!
HUH?
BA (GRAB)
ばっ
WAIT, HOW WERE YOU DOING IT BEFO— MRGH.
GA (SMACK)
YOU SAW HOW AWKWARD IT IS FOR THEM, YEAH? AFTER THE MATCH THEY JUST HAD...
IF WE BECOME FRIENDS, WE'LL SET AN EXAMPLE.
FRRGH!? (HUH!?)

SHE HAS A POINT, I GUESS... DESPITE HER INNOCENT LOOKS, SHE'S REALLY THOUGHTFUL.
ALL RIGHT, I'LL HELP YOU.
YES! COOL!

AHH, THAT FEELS NICE.
WELL, THANKS.
JUST WHAT I'D EXPECT FROM A GIRL WITH YOUNGER SIBLINGS.

HUH? WHEN DID I MENTION THAT?
HEE HEE.

I'VE HEARD SOME THINGS THAT YOU HAVEN'T TALKED ABOUT.
LIKE... YOU'VE GOT A LITTLE REGRET FROM THE NINE SCHOOL COMPETITION, DON'CHA?
HUH...?
WELL, AIRI WAS ACTUALLY PLAYING AROUND WITH THE FLIGHT SPELL RIGHT BEFORE WE CAME.
WHAT!? EVEN THOUGH HER MATCH JUST ENDED ...?
SHE PROBABLY WANTED TO KNOW MORE ABOUT THE SPELL, AND NOT JUST IN THE CONTEXT OF A COMPETITION.
SHE LOOKED LIKE SHE WAS REALLY ENJOYING HERSELF.
...AND YOU...

YOU DECIDED WINNING THE ROOKIE COMPETITION WAS MOST IMPORTANT, SO YOU PURPOSELY DIDN'T DABBLE WITH THE FLIGHT SPELL. AM I RIGHT?
!
WELL ...

I'M SURE YOU'LL ALL BE SURPRISED.
HONOKA?
SO PRETTY...!
BUT...
...I COULDN'T DO IT...

I ACTUALLY WANTED TO GIVE IT A WHIRL MYSELF, BUT THEY STOPPED ME...
ZAAAAA (FSHHHH)
BUT I'M NOT GIVING UP, YOU HEAR? I'M GONNA TRY IT OUT SOON.
IT'S GREAT THAT YOU DIDN'T TAKE A RISK THAT COULD HAVE JEOPARDIZED EVERYTHING...
...BUT YOU DON'T NEED TO HOLD YOURSELF BACK IF YOU REALLY WANT TO TRY IT.
KYU (CLENCH)
WHY NOT ASK HIM FOR AN ARRANGEMENT OF THE SPELL THAT FITS YOU PERSONALLY?
YOU KNOW—THAT ENGINEER YOU'RE SO FOND OF.
......!!!
DOKI (BADUMP)

......
CHAPO (SPLISH)
ちゃぽ
I'M SORRY. TOUKO ALWAYS GETS LIKE THAT...
SHALL I GO SAY SOMETHING?
NO.
HONOKA GETS SWEPT AWAY EASILY, BUT IF SHE DIDN'T LIKE IT, SHE'D REFUSE.

SO I THINK...
...THEY'RE GETTING ALONG...

SHE'S LONELY?

ARE YOU A LONGTIME FRIEND OF MITSUI-SAN'S?
MM. WE'VE ALWAYS COMPETED AGAINST EACH OTHER SINCE ELEMENTARY SCHOOL.

...
WAS I REALLY...
...LOOKING AT HER LIKE THAT?

YES, PRETTY MUCH.
I FIGURED SHE WAS A SPECIAL FRIEND.
...SPECIAL ...
YEAH...

かあああ
KAAAA (BLUSH)
SHE ACTS SO ALOOF AND STRONG...
THIS IS A SURPRISE. MAYBE I SHOULDN'T HAVE...

I'M SHOCKED.
THEY'RE REALLY GETTING ALONG.
TOUKO...
...AND SHIORI...
AS FOR ME...

IT MIGHT BE AWKWARD, BUT I HAVE TO TELL HER...
CHAPTER 71

CAN I SIT A MOMENT?
OF COURSE.
......

...
SO I WAS PRACTICING THE FLIGHT SPELL EARLIER.
WHAT...? WHY?

AFTER GOING AGAINST YOU, I STARTED THINKING I COULD STILL GROW...
...AND THEN I COULDN'T HELP BUT PRACTICE MORE.

REALLY?
YES.

TO BE HONEST, I THOUGHT I WOULD HAVE FELT MUCH MORE CRUSHED AFTER LOSING TO YOU.
BUT STRANGELY, IT FELT LIKE THE WORLD HAD GOTTEN SO MUCH BIGGER... I GOT EXCITED AND REALIZED I WANTED TO SEE WHAT WAS IN THAT NEXT DIMENSION.
WHICH IS WHY...

...I REALLY JUST WANTED TO SAY THIS...
THANK YOU.

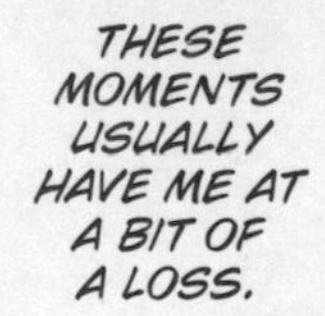
THESE MOMENTS USUALLY HAVE ME AT A BIT OF A LOSS.

THE ONLY THING ON MY MIND DURING THE MATCHES WAS TO WIN...
...TO PROVE THE STRENGTH OF ONII-SAMA'S MAGIC...

...AND TO GIVE HIM A SHOW THAT WOULD MAKE HIM PROUD.

AFTER THE MATCH, WHEN I SEE THE PERSON AGAIN...
...I GET CONFUSED AND START TO WONDER...
...IF I'M BEING ARROGANT WITH MY WORDS AND ATTITUDE...
...AND IF I'M HURTING THEM.

CAN I SIT A MOMENT?
OF COURSE.
SHE'S SMILING, BUT HER EXPRESSION IS A LITTLE STIFF.
IT'S NOT REJECTION, THEN, BUT HESITATION...

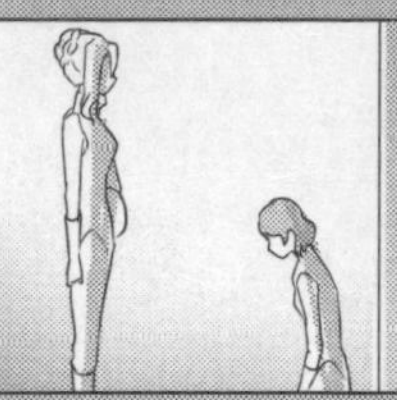

I'VE FELT THAT WAY BEFORE TOO.

SHIBA-SAN PROBABLY HAS SUCH IMMENSE TALENT THAT SHE'S NEVER BEEN IN THE LOSER'S POSITION.
BUT SHE'S TOO NOBLE-MINDED TO TAKE PRIDE IN HER VICTORIES, WHICH MUST CAUSE A LOT OF AWKWARDNESS FOR HER.

THAT'S WHY I JUST HAVE TO TELL HER...
...THAT THOSE SHE PREVAILS OVER AREN'T ONLY DISAPPOINTED...
...BUT THAT THEY'VE ALSO HAD A BEAUTIFUL EXPERIENCE.
I REALLY JUST WANTED TO SAY THIS—THANK YOU.

YOU'RE WELCOME.
I WAS RIGHT ABOUT YOU BEING IN A LEAGUE OF YOUR OWN. NOT EVERY-ONE CAN THINK LIKE THAT—IT'S FRANKLY AMAZING.

YOU'RE THE AMAZING ONE.
I CONSIDER MYSELF LUCKY...
...THAT YOU'RE MY AGE, AND I HAD THE CHANCE TO GO UP AGAINST YOU.
AS DO I.
YOU ARE TRULY STRONG, AND YOU TRIED YOUR HARDEST.
I GREW FROM THAT MATCH TOO, THANKS TO YOU.
REALLY? I'M HONORED TO HEAR THAT.

BY NEXT YEAR, I WILL HAVE GROWN EVEN MORE. I'LL GIVE YOU MORE OF A RUN FOR YOUR MONEY.
OH? WELL, I DON'T INTEND TO LOSE.

HEY! STOP FOOLING AROUND SO MUCH, TOUKO!
OH, JUST LEAVE CEREMONY AT THE DOORSTEP!
バシャ
BASHA (SPLASH)
バシャ
BASHA
WHY?
IS THAT BS MAGIC? FASCINATING...
AH HA HA...

ZA (SHK)
ONII-SAMA!
FUWA (FLOAT)

WELCOME BACK.
I'M SO GLAD YOU'RE SAFE.
SARA (STROKE)
THANKS.

I'M GLAD TO BE BACK.

NADE (PAT)
NADE
ナデナデ
GYU (SQUEEZE)
ぎゅっ

The Honor Student at Magic High School

CHAPTER 72

AT LONG LAST, THE NINE SCHOOL COMPETITION ENDS TOMORROW...

WHICH MEANS...
...TOMORROW IS THE FINAL BATTLE...!

I MUST DANCE WITH TATSUYA-SAN DURING THE POST-CEREMONIES PARTY, NO MATTER WHAT IT TAKES!

BUT TO DO THAT, I'LL NEED TATSUYA-SAN TO FORMALLY REQUEST A DANCE...
...I CAN'T EVEN IMAGINE HIM COMING TO ME FIRST...

WHAT DO YOU THINK...?
HMM... IT'LL BE HARD.
BUOO (WRRR)

I FIGURED YOU'D AGREE...
SIGH...
BUT YOU JUST HAVE TO DO IT.

BE-CAUSE...
...THE PARTY WILL ONLY HAPPEN ONCE!
GASHI (GRAB)
YEAH!?

SHE'S WEIRDLY ENTHUSED ABOUT THIS...
SHIZUKU, REINVIGORATED AFTER THE CONVERSATION LAST NIGHT IN THE BATH TO DO ANYTHING SHE CAN TO HELP HONOKA

STILL, I WONDER IF THERE'S ANYTHING I CAN ACTUALLY DO.
YOU'LL HAVE YOUR CHANCE WHILE WE'RE WATCHING TODAY.
TATSUYA-SAN SHOULD BE FINISHED WITH HIS ENGINEERING JOB FOR THE TOURNAMENT, SO WE'LL BE SPENDING MORE TIME TOGETHER.
THEN, YOU CASUALLY GET CLOSE AND "HAPPEN" TO MENTION THE DANCING AT THE PARTY TO HIM.
I SUPPOSE EVEN HE MIGHT FIGURE IT OUT IF I KEEP TALKING ABOUT IT...
I AM WORRIED ABOUT ONE THING, THOUGH.
HUH ...?

The match is over!
YES! I GRABBED THE SEAT NEXT TO TATSUYA-SAN!
HUH!? I WAS SO ENGROSSED BY THE MATCH AND HIS EXPLANATIONS THAT I DIDN'T HAVE TIME TO BRING UP THE AFTER-PARTY!
WAAA (CHEER)
WAAA
HE JUST USED AN ACCELERATION/ MOVEMENT SPELL WHILE KEEPING "PHALANX" INTACT.
HE REALLY IS INCREDI-BLE...
DOKI
DOKI (BADUM)

GAYA (CHATTER)
GAYA
UMM, HEY, TATSUYA-SA—

OH.
I AM WORRIED ABOUT ONE THING, THOUGH.
HOW MIYUKI WILL REACT...
IS SOMETHING THE MATTER, HONOKA?
SHE WAS RIGHT!
MIYUKI WILL BE ON HER GUARD IF I TALK TO HIM... WELL, FOR NOW...
I-I WAS JUST THINKING WE COULD GO HAVE A SNACK AT ONE OF THE STALLS.
WELL, I AM GETTING A LITTLE HUNGRY.
YES, THAT'S A GOOD IDEA!
I WANT SOME SWEETS.

HOW ABOUT THAT PLACE, THEN?
Japanese Café
THAT LOOKS GOOD.
YES, THAT'S GOOD!

......
I WANTED TO JUMP INTO THE CONVERSATION SO MUCH I ACCIDENTALLY YELLED...

THE WAY JUUMONJI-SENPAI USED "PHALANX" THERE WASN'T THE WAY IT WAS MEANT TO BE USED...
I SEE.
SHIZUKU IS REALLY ENGAGED.

HOW AM I SUPPOSED TO BRING UP THE AFTER-PARTY?

STILL, WITH MIYUKI HERE, I DEFINITELY WON'T BE ABLE TO TELL HIM TO ASK ME TO DANCE...

BUT WHEN WOULD SHE NOT BE AROUND?

BY THE WAY, DID YOU HAVE ANY PLANS AFTER THIS?

I WAS THINKING OF WALKING AROUND WITH MIYUKI FOR A WHILE.
THOUGHT SO...

YES. WE HAVEN'T BEEN ABLE TO SPEND ANY TIME TOGETHER YET, AND WE WANTED AT LEAST ONE DAY.

BUT EXCEPT WHEN HE WAS CHECKING ON OTHER COMPETITORS, YOU TWO WERE STUCK TOGETHER LIKE GLUE!

OH, THAT'S RIGHT... HA-HA.

...IS THIS CHECKMATE !?

COME TO THINK OF IT, THERE'S ALWAYS A DANCE ON THE LAST NIGHT OF THE COMPETITION, RIGHT?
SHIZU-KU!!

DID YOU PLAN ON ASKING ANYONE TO DANCE, TATSUYA-SAN?
EXCLUDING MIYUKI, OF COURSE.

SHOULD I?
I FEEL LIKE I'D BE A NUISANCE ASKING ANYONE TO DANCE, REALLY.
N-NO, NO, YOU WOULDN'T!!
DAN (SLAM)

HONOKA...?
KAA (BLUSH)
かあっ
AH...
I'M SORRY!
IT'S FINE.
......
COULD HONOKA WANT TO...?

THIS WAY!
THAT WAY!
YEAH!
GO FOR IT!
HONOKA...
SHE'S GOING BACK AND FORTH AGAIN.

THE
HONOR
STUDENT
AT
Magic High
School

CHAPTER 73

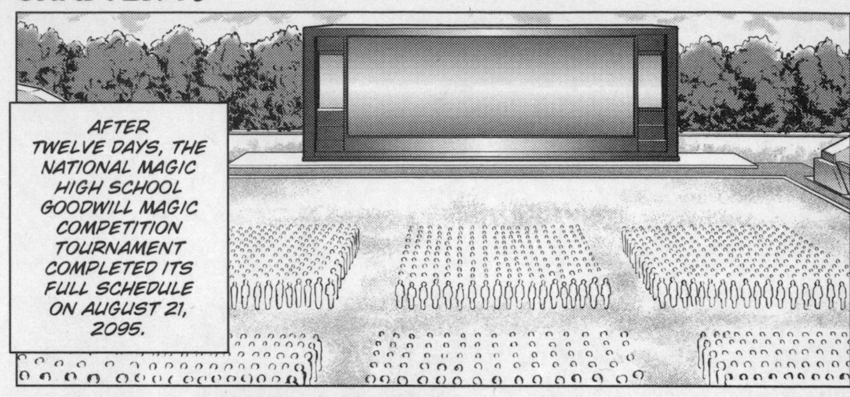

AFTER TWELVE DAYS, THE NATIONAL MAGIC HIGH SCHOOL GOODWILL MAGIC COMPETITION TOURNAMENT COMPLETED ITS FULL SCHEDULE ON AUGUST 21, 2095.

ONCE THE CHAMPIONS OF EACH EVENT WERE AWARDED...

...THE EVENT ENDED "WITHOUT A HITCH."
パチ
PACHI (CLAP)
パチ
PACHI
パチ
PACHI
パチ
PACHI
パチ
PACHI
パチ
PACHI

AND WHEN THE SUN HAD SET...
...A GORGEOUS AFTER-PARTY BEGAN IN THE HOTEL.
ガヤ
GAYA
ガヤ
GAYA (CHATTER)

NIGHT CAME BEFORE I COULD GET OVER MY EMBARRASSMENT AND SAY ANYTHIIING!

I'LL JUST HAVE TO TAKE THE PLUNGE NOW!
LOOK.
THERE'S A MILLION PEOPLE ASKING MIYUKI TO DANCE.
WELL, IT IS MIYUKI!

NOW MIGHT BE YOUR CHANCE...
KA (FLASH)
MIYUKI'S DEFENSES ARE DOWN NOW THAT SHE'S SUR-ROUNDED.
IF YOU TAKE ADVAN-TAGE...
HUH!?
BUT THAT WOULD BE LIKE A SURPRISE ATTACK!
TAJI (FIDGET)
ALL IS FAIR IN LOVE AND WAR.
GO GO GO
GO GO (RUMBLE)
!?

YOU'D GO THAT FAR FOR ME, SHIZUKU? BUT MIYUKI IS A GOOD FRIEND TOO, AND I DON'T WANT TO DO ANYTHING COWARDLY ...

EXCUSE ME. IF YOU WOULDN'T MIND...?

HUH!?

Onii-sama.
KOSO (WHISPER)
Hm?
I THINK HONOKA WANTS YOU TO ASK HER TO DANCE.
SHE DOES?

YES. IT'S TIME TO BE A MAN.

IF YOU SAY SO, MIYUKI.

...!
HE CALLS HER BY HER FIRST NAME!?
MUKA (SNAP)
ムカッ
I'M TERRIBLY SORRY TO INTERRUPT, BUT... SHIBA-SAN, WOULD YOU CARE TO JOIN ME FOR A DANCE?
GUI (EXTEND)
グイ

GO ON, MIYUKI.
IF YOU SAY SO, ONII-SAMA.

WAIT... YOU'RE RELATED!?

YOU DIDN'T REALIZE THAT?

クスッ
KUSU (GIGGLE)
WE DIDN'T LOOK LIKE SIBLINGS TO YOU, DID WE, ICHIJOU-SAN?

HONOKA ...
...WOULD YOU CARE FOR A DANCE?

......!! YES, GLADLY!

GOOD FOR YOU, HONOKA.

GOOD FOR YOU, BUT...

...SEEING ONII-SAMA DANCE WITH OTHER WOMEN...
...MAKES MY CHEST TIGHTEN...

THE HONOR STUDENT AT Magic High School

THE COMPLEXITIES...
...OF A GIRL'S HEART...
I TRULY DO WANT HONOKA TO BE HAPPY, BUT...
SHE'S EVEN BEAUTIFUL WHEN SHE'S ANXIOUS...

CHAPTER 74

IT'S LIKE A DREAM, GETTING TO DANCE WITH SHIBA-SAN ...
HOW BEAUTIFUL...
LIKE A GODDESS...
POWA (GLOW)

BUT...
...I HAD NO IDEA HE WAS HER BROTHER.
HOW COULD I? THEY LOOK NOTHING ALIKE.

STILL, I MAY HAVE BEEN RUDE TO HIM, EVEN THOUGH I DIDN'T KNOW.

I'LL HAVE TO MAKE SURE TO TREAT HIM POLITELY FROM NOW ON.
かぁぁ
KAAA (BLUSH)
THAT WAS EMBARRASSING IN HINDSIGHT...

THANK YOU SO MUCH.

I'D LIKE TO TALK, IF—

わあっ
WAA (ROAR)
ICHIJOU-KUN! ME NEXT!
SHIBA-SAN, WOULD YOU DO ME THE HONOR OF A DANCE?
NO, DO ME THE HONOR!
I THOUGHT I WAS NEXT?
...OF COURSE THAT'S NOT HAPPENING...!

HEE-HEE. MIYUKI-SAN IS PRETTY POPULAR, HUH?
SEEMS LIKE IT.
YOU LOOK SATISFIED. AREN'T YOU JEALOUS?
WHY WOULD I BE JEALOUS?

I'M JUST KIDDING.
SOMETIMES YOU TWO LOOK LIKE LOVERS.
I DON'T APPRECIATE JOKES LIKE THAT. AND I THINK THEY'RE INAPPROPRIATE FOR THE ELDEST DAUGHTER OF THE SAEGUSA.
SORRY. DON'T BRING UP FORMAL STUFF LIKE THAT!
I REALLY AM GRATEFUL TO BOTH OF YOU. WE WOULDN'T HAVE WON THIS YEAR IF NOT FOR YOUR SUPPORT AND MIYUKI-SAN'S STRENGTH.
WE'RE SO FORTUNATE THAT THE TWO OF YOU CAME TO OUR HIGH SCHOOL.
THANK YOU FOR ***ALL THE TIMES*** YOU'VE HELPED US.

......
I'M GRATEFUL TO BE BLESSED WITH SUCH A WONDERFUL PRESIDENT AS WELL.
HMM. IT SOUNDS LIKE YOU'RE PLOTTING SOMETHING!

AND NOW...
YOU WERE CONTACTED TOO, JUUMONJI-KUN?

APPARENTLY THE TEN MASTER CLANS NEED YOU TO CRUSH THE NEXT EVENT—MONOLITH CODE—AS A SHOW OF MIGHT.
RIDICULOUS, ISN'T IT?
MIGHT AS WELL HAVE TATSUYA-KUN AND MIYUKI-SAN...
IF THEY REALLY WERE PART OF THE TEN MASTER CLANS ANYWAY...

AH?
OH.

THANK YOU FOR YESTER-DAY.
WHAT DO YOU MEAN?
MM... I GOT TO GIVE MY FRIEND A LITTLE PUSH, THANKS TO YOU.
OHHH! SHE FINALLY CONFESSED HER FEELINGS?
WELL, NOT YET.

...BUT THE SUMMER IS JUST GETTING STARTED!
GOOOO (ROAR)
...SO THIS IS WHO SHE REALLY IS.
TRULY SURPRISING...

OH RIGHT. LET'S TRADE NUMBERS.
I DECIDED TO STUDY ABROAD NEXT SEMESTER.
THAT'S AWFULLY SUDDEN!
YOU DIDN'T KNOW EITHER?
I ONLY DECIDED TO DO IT RECENTLY.

THIS COMPETITION WAS JUST SO EXCITING.
IT'S A JOURNEY TO PERFECT MY SKILLS!

I PROBABLY WON'T BE BACK FOR A WHILE, SO LET ME TEXT YOU WHEN I'M LONELY.
OKAY.
SHOULD I TELL HONOKA AND MIYUKI TOO?
YES, PLEASE!
THEY'RE EVEN FRIENDLIER NOW...

TATSUYA-KUN! YOU'RE DANCING WITH ME NEXT.
DON (BAM)

I'M SORRY, BUT PRESIDENT SAEGUSA, SHE...
SHE WORE ME OUT...
YOU WOULDN'T BE RUDE ENOUGH TO REJECT AN INVITATION FROM A WOMAN, WOULD YOU?
......

IS THAT WATA-NABE-SENPAI?
ONII-SAMA IS WITH ANOTHER WOMAN...
NO, I CAN'T. HE SHOULD NATURALLY BE POPULAR WITH EVERYONE. I SHOULD BE HAPPY ABOUT IT.

BUT IT STILL HURTS.

THIS TIME, I'LL GET HIM—
KYORO (TURN)
きょろ
SHIBA-SAN, PLEASE DANCE WITH ME!

CHIRA (GLANCE)
ちらっ
AH...
G-GLADLY...
NO CHOICE ...

NEXT TIME FOR SURE—
SHIBA-SAN!
NEXT TIME—
I CAN'T. NOW HE'S TALKING TO JUUMONJI-SENPAI.
WHEN AM I GOING TO BE ABLE TO DANCE WITH HIM...?

HO-HO!
POWERFUL ENEMIES APPEAR BEFORE TATSUYA...!
WA-HA-HA!
BAAAN (BAAAM)
...

CHAPTER 75

OH, MIZUKI, WHAT'S THIS?
XX-XXXX-XXXX
(NUMBER)
A STUDENT FROM ANOTHER SCHOOL LEFT IT ON THE TRAY...
WHAT!?
MIZUKI, GO WASH DISHES FOR A WHILE! YOU TOO, MIKIHIKO!
BI (POINT)
MIKI, IT'S YOUR FAULT FOR NOT WATCHING, YOU KNOW!
DON'T CALL ME MIKI!
STOP IT WITH THAT!
I DO APOLOGIZE FOR NOT BEING ATTENTIVE ENOUGH, THOUGH...

NO, I COULDN'T!
HEY, YOU, LET'S GO.
IT'S FINE! WE'LL HANDLE CLEANING UP THE BALLROOM!
WAIT, ME TOO?
OH, I SEE. GOTCHA.

GAH...
EEE!♥

ダッ
DA (DASH)

SIGH.

AH, CRAP!
I DIDN'T WANT TO SEE THAT WOMAN'S FACE!

HUH?
TATSUYA-KUN?

OH?

JUUMONJI-KUN AND TATSUYA-KUN?

MIGHT AS WELL HAVE TATSUYA-KUN AND MIYUKI-SAN...
YEAH. WITH MAGICIANS AS POWERFUL AS THEM, THEY MIGHT MARRY INTO THE TEN MASTER CLANS.

JUU-MONJI-KUN, YOU'RE NOT...?
OH, THERE YOU ARE, PRINCESS.

YOU SEEM TO BE FITTING THE ROLE OF PRINCE QUITE WELL, MARI.
DID YOU DANCE WITH YOUR FANGIRLS?
YEAH.
AND THEN...
...I DANCED WITH TATSUYA-KUN TOO.
YOU DID?
YOU REALLY DID A NUMBER ON HIM!
I'VE NEVER SEEN HIM SO EXHAUSTED. IT WAS PRETTY FUNNY.
WELL, EXCUSE ME.
MAYBE, DESPITE HIS LOOKS, HE LACKS STAMINA.
HEH.
IT'S PROBABLY HIS FIRST AND LAST TIME DANCING WITH YOU, MAYUMI. THAT'S SURE TO BE SOMETHING TO LOOK BACK ON.

RIGHT. WE'RE GRADUATING AFTER THIS ONE, AREN'T WE?
IT WAS A PRETTY GOOD HIGH SCHOOL EXPERIENCE.
......
OH, ABOUT TATSUYA-KUN...

YES, VERY.

SO THIS WAS MY LAST NINE SCHOOL COMPETI-TION...

AND THE FINAL TIME I COULD GO OUT THERE WITH YOU. WHAT HAP-PENED DURING MIRAGE BAT WAS A LITTLE UNFORTU-NATE.
WHAT ARE YOU SAYING? IT WAS UNFORTUNATE FOR BOTH OF US.
MORE IMPORTANTLY, THOUGH, YOU'RE HAPPY THE WORLD SEEMS SO MUCH BIGGER NOW, AREN'T YOU?

!
...YOU REALLY DO SEE THROUGH EVERY-THING.

YOU'RE GONNA KEEP ON GROWING, AIRI.
I'LL SHOW YOU SOMETHING EVEN BETTER NEXT YEAR.
KOKU (NOD)
コクッ
LOOKING FORWARD TO IT. I'LL BE THERE!
SEEING AIRI GROW MAKES ME HAPPY.

AND IF I CAN ONE DAY HELP SUPPORT HER RADIANCE...

SHE'S THE ELEMENT GIRL.

WHAT IF MY FEELINGS ABOUT AIRI'S GROWTH BEING SO RADIANT ARE NOTHING MORE THAN A PRODUCT OF MY TRAITS AS AN ELEMENT?
...IT'S SOMETHING I'VE THOUGHT ABOUT BEFORE.

I WONDER IF SHE WORRIES ABOUT THE SAME THING...

MIYUKI... SHE'S LOOKING FOR TATSUYA-SAN...?

SHE PROBABLY STILL HASN'T DANCED WITH HIM.
AND YET HE ASKED ME TO...
I'M SORRY, MIYUKI.
I REALLY LIKE MIYUKI TOO.
SHE'S PROUD, AND BEAUTIFUL, AND JUST WONDERFUL.
I REALLY LIKE TATSUYA-SAN, BUT MIYUKI IS ALSO A PRECIOUS FRIEND TO ME.
I WANT TO HELP HER GET HER WISH TOO.

BUT THE FIRST PROBLEM IS HOW SHE CAN'T GET AWAY FROM THE CONSTANT STREAM OF PEOPLE ASKING HER TO DANCE.
SHE'D NEVER TURN THEM DOWN...
MASAKI, GOT A SEC?
GEORGE!
SORRY, GOTTA STEP AWAY...
HUH?
OH!

THAT'S RIGHT! I JUST HAVE TO INTERRUPT!
GREAT!
WAIT! NOW THAT I THINK ABOUT IT, I DON'T KNOW WHERE TATSUYA-SAN IS...
I DON'T WANT TO BE WAN-DERING AROUND WITH HER.
OH NO, OH NO...
AND THE DANCING TIME IS ALMOST OVER!
MIGHT YOU BE SEARCHING FOR SOMETHING, MISS?
ERIKA!

CHAPTER 76

ERIKA MIGHT KNOW— SHE'S BEEN ALL OVER THE VENUE!
ERIKA, HAVE YOU SEEN TATSUYA-SAN?

I SAW HIM HEADING TO THE CENTRAL COURTYARD EARLIER WITH JUUMONJI-SENPAI.

REALLY!? THANKS, ERIKA!
THANK GOOD-NESS...
DID SOMETHING HAPPEN?
WELL...

MIYUKI!

PHEW...
SU (CALM)
ス

SHUN (DROOP)
しゅん…
ZORO (SHUFFLE)
ゾロ
ZORO
ゾロ…

THANK YOU FOR BEFORE.
YOU TOLD TATSUYA-SAN TO COME TO ME, RIGHT?

I CAN'T BELIEVE HE TOLD YOU.

HEE HEE.
WELL, HE'S A GOOD PERSON.

LOOK, THE DANCE IS ALMOST OVER.
YOU HAVE TO DANCE WITH HIM.
I'D LOVE TO, BUT...
MISS...
...YOUR COMPANION IS RIGHT THIS WAY.
SHE SAID HE'S IN THE CENTRAL COURTYARD.
......!!

THANK YOU, ERIKA! HONOKA!

THANKS FOR THE SAVE.
TOUGH BEING POPULAR, HUH?
NAH...
THOUGH I GUESS ...

...THEY EXPECT AS MUCH FROM ME—OR RATHER, FROM THE *ICHIJOU*.
I HAVE TO DO MY BEST TO MEET THOSE EXPECTATIONS.
FOR YOUR PRIDE AS PART OF THE CLANS?

YEAH.
KOKU (NOD)
コク

WE MAY GO TO DIFFERENT SCHOOLS, BUT SAEGUSA AND JUUMONJI ARE PROBABLY UNDER THE SAME PRESSURE.
AND I WANT TO BE ABLE TO STAND AS EQUALS WITH THEM.

WELL, YOU'LL ALWAYS HAVE MY SUPPORT.
THANKS, GEORGE.
I'LL BE COUNTING ON YOU.

COME TO THINK OF IT, SHIBA—ER, THE ONE WHO COMPETED IN MONOLITH CODE...
WELL...
?

WHAT ABOUT HIM?
DID YOU KNOW HE WAS SHIBA-SAN'S OLDER BROTHER?

HUH!?
YOU MEAN HE DIDN'T KNOW!?
OH... HE, UH, HE WAS?

I KNEW IT! YOU WEREN'T AWARE EITHER, WERE YOU?
THEY LOOK NOTHING ALIKE, AFTER ALL!
PAAA (BEAM)
ぱぁあ
ER... YEAH...
HE'S... SUCH AN AIRHEAD.

THE REASON I'M DRAWN TO MASAKI...
...ISN'T JUST BECAUSE HE'S GREAT, OR BECAUSE HE SAVED ME.

MAYBE THIS IS WHAT I REALLY LIKE ABOUT HIM.

ER, NOT IN A WEIRD WAY OR ANY-THING...

PIKA (GLOW)
ピ
カッ
GLOW OF
HONESTY
EVEN IN THIS ENVIRONMENT, HE KEEPS THE SAME PERSONALITY...
I THINK THAT'S AMAZING...

THE
HONOR
STUDENT
AT
Magic High
School

CHAPTER 77

JUUMONJI-SENPAI, ISN'T THE BANQUET ABOUT TO START?
IT WON'T TAKE LONG.
SHIBA, YOU TWO...
YOU'RE IN THE TEN MASTER CLANS, AREN'T YOU?
NO.

I AM NOT PART OF THE CLANS.
I SEE... IN THAT CASE...

DOES HE SUSPECT US? IF IT SEEMS LIKE HE'LL HARM MIYUKI, THEN...

...HOW ABOUT SAEGUSA?
WHAT?

SHE HAS A LOT OF CUTE ASPECTS TO HER...
ZAAAA (FSHHHH)
ザアァァ
WHAT IS HE TALKING ABOUT...?

A STRATEGIC MARRIAGE TO GET SHIBA INTO THE TEN MASTER CLANS!?
ONLY JUUMONJI...
HE'S GOT AN OLD MAN'S—ER, A WAY OF THINKING BEYOND HIS YEARS.
YEAH, BUT HE DOESN'T MEAN ANYTHING BY IT.

HE'S IMPORTANT ENOUGH TO ADVISE THE JUUMONJI'S REPRESENTATIVE AT THE CLANS CONFERENCE...
...SO HE VIEWS THIS AS DOING WHATEVER IT TAKES TO PROTECT THE LARGER ORDER.

HIS DEFEAT OF THE NEXT HEAD OF THE ICHIJOU...
...IS ACTUALLY CAUSING A STIR AT THE CLANS CONFERENCE...
RIGHT, THAT... WAIT, WASN'T JUUMONJI THE ONE WHO PUT HIM UP TO IT?
WE DID TOO, BUT...

WELL, CAN'T BLAME HIM.
YOU CAN TRY TO PASS OFF A GEM AS A PEBBLE, BUT SOMEONE'S BOUND TO FIND OUT EVENTU-ALLY.
MM-HMM.

OUR TIME AS STUDENTS WON'T LAST FOREVER.
EVENTUALLY, EVERYONE WILL HAVE TO CHOOSE THEIR OWN FUTURES BASED ON THEIR POSITION AND TALENTS.

STILL...
IT MIGHT BE THAT THE MORE TALENTED YOU ARE, THE MORE IT CHAINS YOU DOWN.
BUT MAYBE THOSE TWO CAN...

OH...
JUUMONJI-SENPAI.
WHICH MEANS ONII-SAMA IS HERE!
TA (DASH)
ONII-SAMA!
MIYUKI?

I'VE BEEN LOOKING ALL OVER FOR YOU!
OH? I'M SORRY.
BUT YOU SHOULDN'T RUN LIKE THAT AT NIGHT.
YES...

DID JUUMONJI-SENPAI HAVE SOMETHING IMPORTANT TO TALK ABOUT?
NO, IT WAS NOTHING MUCH.
HONESTLY.
IT'S A GOOD THING MIYUKI DIDN'T HEAR THAT.
GOOOOO (RUMBLE)
PROGNOSTIC

THAT SONG ...
THE LAST DANCE IS ABOUT TO BEGIN...
ONII-SAMA.
SU (SLIP)

HAA.
HAA.
MAY I HAVE THIS DANCE?
CERTAINLY.

I WISH...

...THIS MOMENT WOULD LAST FOREVER...

* TATSUYA IS WEARING
A BORROWED BLAZER.

THE
HONOR
STUDENT
AT
Magic High
School

FINAL CHAPTER

YAAAY!
Heh-heh!
Due to my special training on the raging ocean waves, you will witness my improvement the next time we meet!
This is just you playing.
Huh?
Nooo, I won't lose!
Ha-ha.
Touko gets stronger from playing.
It... certainly seems like it.
We should get stronger by playing too, Shizuku!
Ahh, you two want to come for special training in the ocean with me?
Yeah! We can go to Shizuku's summer house!
We get good waves.

That sounds great! You should invite us sometime!
You'd be welcome to come, of course.
YES— NOW I UNDER-STAND.
With love, Mom
WHY MOM RAN FROM HOME...
...AND CAME TO JAPAN.

WOW, ALL YOUR SWIMSUITS LOOK SO CUTE!
THEY'RE PRETTY BOLD...
WE'RE IN HIGH SCHOOL, SO MAYBE I SHOULD PICK SOMETHING MORE MATURE.

AND THEN TATSUYA-SAN WILL...
POOO (GAZE)
LIKE WHAT YOU SEE?

EXCUSE ME.
BIKU (TWITCH)
ACK!

ARE YOU TWO MAGIC HIGH SCHOOL STUDENTS?

MY DAUGHTER ACTUALLY SAW THE NINE SCHOOL COMPETITION ON TV THE OTHER DAY AND DECIDED TO TRY AND GET INTO A MAGIC HIGH SCHOOL HERSELF.
U-UMM... CAN I SHAKE YOUR HAND?
SURE THING!

EH-HEH-HEH! I FEEL LIKE A CELEBRITY.
WELL, THE COMPETITION BROADCAST IS PRETTY POPULAR.
I WATCHED IT WHEN I WAS LITTLE TOO.

THANK YOU FOR DELIVERING THE REPORT TO THE BRANCH OFFICE, ONII-SAMA.
NO PROBLEM.
I HEARD OUR AUNT COMPLI-MENTED YOU ON THE NINE SCHOOL COMPETI-TION TOO.
OH! IS THAT RIGHT?
I'M HONESTLY NOT SURE WHAT SHE'S THINKING—WASN'T SHE THE ONE WHO SAID NOT TO DO ANYTHING TOO CONSPICUOUS?

! SOMEONE'S WATCHING US.
EXCUSE ME...!
YOU'RE THE LADY FROM THAT FIRE, RIGHT?
I'VE ALWAYS WANTED TO THANK YOU FOR SAVING ME.
OH...

SO THANK YOU VERY MUCH!
PEKO (BOW)
YOU'RE VERY WELCOME. I'M HAPPY TO SEE YOU SAFE.

POOOO (GAAAAZE)
ぽー
OH!
JI (STARE)
じっ
WHY IS THAT MAN STARING AT ME LIKE THAT...?

OH! IT'S BECAUSE I INTER-RUPTED THEIR DATE!
I GUESS THAT MAKES SENSE. SHE'S SO PRETTY, AFTER ALL.
I'M SORRY FOR INTERRUPTING YOUR DATE!
PLEASE DON'T MIND ME.
SU (SHF) ス
SU ス

SHE'S PRETTY MATURE FOR A KID.
MIYUKI—
デート
DATE

LET'S TAKE OUR SWEET TIME ON OUR DATE TODAY, ONII-SAMA.
IT'S BEEN A LONG TIME SINCE I'VE BEEN TO YOKOHAMA.
MM. YOUR WISH IS MY COMMAND.

FIN

WHER-EVER I AM, AS LONG AS IT'S WITH YOU...
...I'M HAPPY...

THANK YOU SO MUCH FOR THESE PAST EIGHT YEARS.
THE OPPORTUNITY TO WORK ON THIS SERIES AND GETTING TO DRAW EVERYONE FROM MAGIC HIGH SCHOOL FOR SO LONG ARE IRREPLACEABLE TREASURES TO ME!
I'LL KEEP ROOTING FOR THE MAGIC HIGH SCHOOL SERIES IN THE FUTURE!
YU MORI

Special Thanks!
SATO-SENSEI ISHIDA-SAMA JIMMY STONE-SAMA
ISHIMOTO-SAMA TOMIYAMA-SAMA
ASADA-SAMA KOBAYASHI-SAMA TANAKA-SAMA
KANEKO-SAMA MIZUTA-SAMA ENDOU-SAMA
KITANO-SAMA MURAYAMA-SAMA
AND THANK YOU TO EVERYONE WHO READ ALL THE WAY TO THE END!!

Glossary

Activation sequence
The blueprints for magic and the programs used to construct it. Activation sequence data is stored in a compressed format in C.A.D.s. Design waves are sent from the magician to the device, where they're converted into a signal according to the decompressed data and returned to the magician.

Blanche
A national anti-magic political organization with the objective of uprooting discrimination in society based on magical ability. They hold protest activities based on the criticism of the fictional concept of the current system giving special political treatment to magicians. Behind the scenes, they engage in terrorism and other illegal activities and are strictly watched by the public peace agency.

Blooms, Weeds
Terms representing the gap between Course 1 students and Course 2 students in First High. The left breast of Course 1 student uniforms is emblazoned with an eight-petaled emblem, but it is absent from Course 2 uniforms.

Cabinet
A small, linear vehicle holding either two or four passengers and controlled by a central station. Used for commuting to work and school as a public transportation replacement for trains.

Cardinal George
Shinkurou Kichijouji's nickname. Given to him for having discovered one of the Cardinal Codes, which only existed in theory beforehand, at the young age of thirteen.

Cast jamming
A variety of typeless magic that obstructs magic sequences from exerting influence on Eidos. It weakens the process by which magic sequences affect Eidos by scattering large amounts of meaningless psionic waves.

C.A.D. (Casting Assistant Device)
A device that simplifies the activation of magic. Magical programming is recorded inside. The main types are specialized and multipurpose.

Crimson Prince
Masaki Ichijou's nickname. Given to him for having fought through a battle "drenched in the blood of enemy and ally alike" during the Sado Invasion of 2092 as a volunteer soldier on the defensive line at the young age of thirteen.

Eidos (Individual information body)
Originally a term from Greek philosophy. In modern magic, Eidos are the bodies of information that accompany phenomena. They record the existence of those phenomena on the world, so they can also be called the footprints phenomena leave on the world. The definition of "magic" in modern magic refers to the technology that modifies these phenomena by modifying Eidos.

Four Leaves Technology (F.L.T.)
A domestic C.A.D. manufacturer. Originally famous for its magic engineering products, rather than finished C.A.D.s, but with the development of its Silver line of models, its fame skyrocketed as a C.A.D. manufacturer.

Idea (Information body dimension)
Pronounced "ee-dee-ah." Originally a term from Greek philosophy. In modern magic, "Idea" refers to the platform on which Eidos are recorded. Magic's primary form is a technology wherein a magic sequence is output onto this platform, thus rewriting the Eidos recorded within.

Loopcast system
Activation sequences made so a magician can continually execute a spell as many times as their calculation capacity will permit. Normally, one must re-expand activation sequences from the C.A.D. every time one executes the same spell, but the loopcast system makes it possible by automatically duplicating the activation sequence's final state in the magician's magic calculation region.

Magician
An abbreviation of "magical technician," referring to anyone with the skill to use magic at a practical level.

Magic Association of Japan
A social group of Japanese magicians based in Kyoto. The Kantou branch location is established within Yokohama Bay Hills Tower.

Magic calculation region
A mental region for construction of magic sequences. The substance, so to speak, of magical talent.
It exists in a magician's unconscious, and even if a magician is normally aware of using his or her magic calculation region, he or she cannot be aware of the processes being conducted within. The magic calculation region can be called a "black box" for the magician him- or herself.

Magic engineer
Refers to engineers who design, develop, and maintain apparatuses that assist, amplify, and strengthen magic. Their reputation in society is slightly worse than that of magicians. However, magic engineers are indispensable for tuning C.A.D.s, indispensable tools for magicians, so in the industrial world, they're in higher demand than normal magicians. A first-rate magic engineer's earnings surpass even that of first-rate magicians.

Magic high school
The nickname for the high schools affiliated with the National Magic University. There are nine established throughout the country. Of them, the first through the third have two hundred students per grade and use the Course 1/Course 2 system.

Magic sequence
An information body for the purpose of temporarily altering information attached to phenomena. They are constructed from the psions possessed by magicians.

Nine School Competition
An abbreviation of "National Magic High School Goodwill Magic Competition Tournament." Magic high school students across the country, from First through Ninth High, are gathered to compete with their schools in fierce magic showdowns. There are six events: Speed Shooting, Cloudball, Battle Board, Ice Pillars Break, Mirage Bat, and Monolith Code.

"Program Demolition"
A typeless spell that fires a mass of compressed psionic particles directly into a target without going through the Idea, then causes them to explode, making any psionic information bodies with recorded magic attached to the target, such as activation or magic sequences, scatter. It is technically a spell, but as it is a psion bullet without the structure needed to be a magic sequence and alter events, it isn't affected by things like Information Boost or "Area Interference." In addition, the bullet's inherent pressure repels the effects of cast jamming. Because it has zero physical effect, no sort of obstacle is able to block it.

"Program Dispersion"
A spell that disperses a magic sequence, magic's main form, into psionic particles without a meaningful structure. Because a magic sequence affects information bodies incident to events, its information structure must necessarily be exposed, meaning there is no method to prevent interference with the magic sequence itself. On the other hand, one needs to be able to perceive the magic sequence's construction in order to dismantle it. As spells can be completely activated within fractions of a second in modern magic, one would need a unique information-processing ability able to perceive the structure of magic sequences and analyze them before the magic activates simply by "looking" at them. This has been achieved in experiments where a person knows the spell to be used in advance, but it is widely thought to be impossible to put into practical use.

Psions
Non-physical particles belonging to the dimension of psychic phenomena, psions are elements that record information on consciousness and thought products. Eidos—the theoretical basis for modern magic—as well as activation sequences and magic sequences—supporting its main framework—are all bodies of information constructed from psions. Also referred to as "thought particles."

Pushions (Psycheons)
Non-physical particles belonging to the dimension of psychic phenomena. Their existence has been proven, but their true form and functions have yet to be elucidated. Magicians are generally only able to "feel" the pushions being activated through magic. Also referred to as "spirit particles."

Tactical-class magician
A magician who can use tactical-class magic—magic with the power to destroy an entire city or fleet in a single attack. Thirteen such tactical magicians have been made internationally public, and these are called the Thirteen Apostles.

Taurus Silver
A magic engineer at Four Leaps Technology whose real name, face, and profile have not been made public. His various achievements have led to rapid advances in all aspects of magic technology.

The Ten Master Clans
The strongest group of magicians in Japan. Ten families from a list of twenty-eight are chosen during the Ten Master Clans Selection Conference, which happens every four years, and are named as the Ten Master Clans. The twenty-eight families are Ichijou, Ichinokura, Isshiki, Futatsugi, Nikaidou, Nihei, Mitsuya, Mikazuki, Yotsuba, Itsuwa, Gotou, Itsumi, Mutsuzuka, Rokkaku, Rokugou, Roppongi, Saegusa, Shippou, Tanabata, Nanase, Yatsushiro, Hassaku, Hachiman, Kudou, Kuki, Kuzumi, Juumonji, and Tooyama.

THE HONOR STUDENT AT MAGIC HIGH SCHOOL 11

YU MORI
Original Story: TSUTOMU SATO
Character Design: KANA ISHIDA

Translation: Andrew Prowse
Lettering: Phil Christie

Yen Press
150 West 30th Street, 19th Floor
New York, NY 10001

Visit us at yenpress.com
facebook.com/yenpress
twitter.com/yenpress
yenpress.tumblr.com
instagram.com/yenpress

First Yen Press Edition: June 2021

Yen Press is an imprint of Yen Press, LLC.
The Yen Press name and logo are trademarks of Yen Press, LLC.

The publisher is not responsible for websites (or their content) that are not owned by the publisher.

Library of Congress Control Number: 2016932699

ISBNs: 978-1-9753-2526-8 (paperback)
978-1-9753-2527-5 (ebook)

10 9 8 7 6 5 4 3 2 1

WOR

Printed in the United States of America